Published by Creative Education
P.O. Box 227, Mankato, Minnesota 56002
Creative Education is an imprint of The Creative Company

Design and production by Blue Design
Printed in the United States of America

Photographs by Getty Images (Andrew D. Bernstein, Bernstein Associates, Walter Bibikow, David Bolly/MLB Photos, Jonathan Daniel, Jonathan Daniel/Allsport, Diamond Images, Stephen Dunn, David Durochik/MLB Photos, FPG, David L. Green/MLB Photos, Jose Jimenez/Primera Hora, Jonathan Krin/Allsport, Mitchell Layton, Mitchell Layton/MLB Photos, Rob Leiter/MLB Photos, National Baseball Hall of Fame Library/MLB Photos, John Phillips//Time Life Pictures, Rich Pilling/MLB Photos, Arnold Sachs, Ezra Shaw, Robert Skeoch/MLB Photos, Don Smith/MLB Photos, Ron Vesely/MLB Photos), National Baseball Hall of Fame Library, Cooperstown, N.Y

Library of Congress Cataloging-in-Publication Data

Hawkes, Brian.
The story of the Washington Nationals / by Brian Hawkes.
p. cm. — (Baseball: the great American game)
Includes index.
ISBN-13: 978-1-58341-553-5
1. Washington Nationals (Baseball team)—History—Juvenile literature. I. Title. II. Series.

GV875.W27H39 2007
796.357'6409753—dc22   2006027461

First Edition
9 8 7 6 5 4 3 2 1

Cover: Third baseman Ryan Zimmerman
Page 1: Pitcher Livan Hernandez
Page 3: Outfielder Jose Guillen

THE STORY OF THE
WASHINGTON NATIONALS

by Brian Hawkes

THE STORY OF THE
Washington Nationals

Big right fielder Larry Walker and ace pitcher Pedro Martinez had the Montreal faithful dancing in their seats throughout the 1994 season, believing it was finally going to be the Expos' year. Walker's potent bat struck fear into opposing pitchers, while Martinez's menacing glare and powerful arm bewildered hitters. By August 11, the talented team was six games ahead of the Atlanta Braves in the divisional race and primed to contend for the world championship. Unfortunately, on August 12, 1994, major-league players went on strike, forcing a premature end to the season. The heartsick Expos never recovered. Over the next 10 seasons, the Expos found little success on the field. As the number of fans in the stands dwindled, it became obvious that the team needed a new home. In 2005, the Montreal Expos moved to Washington, D.C., and became the Nationals. While the team's home and name were new, the goal remained the same—to win a first World Series.

THE EXPOS COME TO TOWN

In 1535, French explorer Jacques Cartier sailed down the St. Lawrence River in Canada and discovered an island dominated by a large green hill. He named the place Montreal. More than 100 years later, French missionaries settled on the island and attempted to bring Christianity to the Native Americans. By the late 1600s, Montreal had become a key city in New France. Although France surrendered the city to Great Britain in 1760, to this day, Montreal has retained much of its French heritage.

Over the next 200 years, Montreal prospered. In 1967, the cosmopolitan city hosted a giant world's fair known as the Exposition, or Expo for short. The event attracted widespread attention—even from American Major League Baseball officials. Baseball was seeking to expand by two franchises in 1969. When Montreal submitted an official bid for a team in 1968, the question was whether or not its hockey-crazed citizens would support a baseball franchise. Baseball officials decided to

GEORGES BAREAU

JACQUES CARTIER

MONTREAL

MONTREAL – The second-largest city in Canada, Montreal is known for its rich history and architecture. The largely French-speaking city has also long been known for its National Hockey League team, the Canadiens, which has won 26 world championships.

BASEBALL IN WASHINGTON

Before the Nationals came to town, the Washington Senators were the first big-league team to play baseball in the nation's capital. From 1901 to 1961, the Senators were an American League (AL) franchise. Because they finished in last place four times in their first nine seasons, fans had a saying about them: "First in war, first in peace, and last in the American League." The emergence of Hall of Fame starting pitcher Walter Johnson proved to be the catalyst the team needed to escape from the cellar, and in both 1912 and 1913, the Senators finished in second place. In 1924, the surprising Senators, led by 27-year-old player/manager Bucky Harris, won a world

championship—the only one in team history. Over the next 10 years, the team won two more AL pennants, but from 1934 to 1961, the Senators had only four more winning seasons. The team's lack of success prompted ownership to relocate the franchise to Minnesota, creating the Minnesota Twins, and an expansion franchise also known as the Washington Senators was immediately awarded to the D.C. area. For the next 10 years, the new Washington Senators struggled to build a fan base, and after the 1971 season, they relocated to Dallas and became the Texas Rangers.

take a chance on the city, though, and granted Montreal a major-league team. On October 14, 1968, an expansion draft was conducted, allowing the newest members of the National League (NL), the Montreal Expos and San Diego Padres, to choose players from existing teams to fill out their rosters. Among the Expos' picks were pitchers Dan McGinn and Bill Stoneman.

The Expos entered their first season led by veteran skipper Gene Mauch. Mauch, known as the "Little General," was a disciplined man who worked his players hard during spring training. "At the end of each day, I felt like an old sock in a washing machine," grumbled one tired Expos outfielder. On April 8, 1969, the Expos played their first game against the New York Mets at Shea Stadium in New York. In the third inning, the left-handed McGinn hit the first home run for the new team, and the Expos went on to win the game 11–10. On April 14, the Expos beat the St. Louis Cardinals 8–7 in their home opener at Jarry Park, and three days later, Stoneman tossed the first no-hitter in Expos history against the Philadelphia Phillies.

Still, like most expansion teams, the Montreal Expos struggled in their inaugural season. The team finished 52–110, but the losses didn't keep the Montreal faithful from coming out to support *Nos Amours*, French for "our beloveds." On the contrary, more than 1.2 million spectators visited Jarry Park that year. Encouraged by the fan support, right fielder Rusty Staub—whose fiery red hair earned him the nickname "Le Grande Orange"—led the club up the NL Eastern Division standings in 1970. Rookie pitching sensation Carl Morton did his part as well, winning 18 games and claiming NL Rookie of the Year honors. The team finished the year a dramatically improved 73–89.

The Expos made steady progress throughout the early 1970s. In 1973, pitcher Steve Rogers was called up from the minor leagues and helped the Expos stay in the pennant race until the last few weeks of the season, and they finished three and a half games behind the New York Mets. "Wait until next year," proclaimed Mauch. "These guys are just getting started." Mauch's bold prediction was based on the knowledge that a talented group of youngsters was about to make its mark. In 1974, Gary "Kid" Carter made his major-league debut as an outfielder, and Larry Parrish came on board as a third baseman. But Mauch did not stay long enough to see these players become stars. After he left, Montreal slipped to a disastrous 55–107 finish in 1976, and Expos owners decided it was time for a change.

RUSTY STAUB — Staub attained two career highs in 1970, clubbing 30 home runs with his choppy swing and eking out 12 stolen bases. The redheaded fan favorite played in Montreal from 1969 to 1971 and later returned for part of the 1979 season.

PITCHER • STEVE ROGERS

A crafty right-handed starter, Rogers is widely regarded as the best pitcher in Expos history. A late bloomer, he didn't even play baseball until his senior year in high school. Rogers spent his entire 13-year career with the Expos, winning 158 games. While he was never able to win 20 games in a single season, he did win 19 games in 1982 and posted winning records in eight seasons. Rogers will forever be remembered as the man who gave up the series-winning home run to the Los Angeles Dodgers' Rick Monday in the 1981 NLCS, but his accomplishments as an Expos player spoke for themselves.

STATS

Expos seasons: 1973–85

Height: 6-1

Weight: 182

- **129 complete games**

- **37 complete-game shutouts**

- **158–152 career record**

- **5-time All-Star**

STEVE ROGERS
PITCHER

WASHINGTON NATIONALS

HAIL TO THE CHIEF

On April 14, 1910, the Washington Senators opened their season with 12,000 fans in attendance. Among those fans was William Taft, the 27th president of the United States. Prior to the game, umpire Billy Evans walked over to the president, handed him a ball, and instructed him to throw out the ceremonial first pitch from his seat. Taft threw the ball to starting pitcher Walter Johnson and stayed for the entire game, watching Johnson pitch a one-hit shutout. President Taft started a tradition of the nation's "chief" attending opening day in the capital city. Prior to the Senators' move to Texas in 1972, each president after Taft attended opening day at least once. Presidents Taft and Woodrow Wilson brought good luck to the Senators; the team went a combined 5–0 in games they attended. On the other hand, presidents Richard Nixon and Lyndon Johnson brought nothing but bad luck to the Senators, who went a combined 0–5 in games they attended. Since 1972, the tradition of presidents and opening day has continued in other major-league cities. To date, the only president never to throw out a ceremonial first pitch was Jimmy Carter.

NATIONALS

[13]

BUILDING A CONTENDER

In 1977, new manager Dick Williams took over, and the club moved to the domed Olympic Stadium. One of Williams's first decisions was to name Carter his everyday catcher. Carter took the position shift in stride, saying, "If you put your mind to it, you can achieve what you want. Ambition has always been a motivating force in my life." And Carter's ambition was to turn the Expos into winners. While Carter was growing into his new role as team leader, center fielder Andre "The Hawk" Dawson, who had broken into the major leagues late in the 1976 season, hit 19 home runs and stole 21 bases, hinting at a great career to come.

Behind Carter and Dawson, the Expos started coming together. In 1979, the club had its sights set on an NL Eastern Division title and the first playoff berth in team history. On June 17, Carter was part of a trio of Expos (along with first baseman Tony Perez and outfielder Ellis Valentine) who hit back-to-back-to-back home runs for the first time in team history. With a potent lineup and a talented pitching staff led by Rogers, the Expos contended with the Phillies until the last week of the season. Although the Phillies won the division, the Expos

Although most famous for his booming bat, Andre Dawson won eight Gold Glove awards for his defense.

ANDRE DAWSON

CATCHER · GARY CARTER

Nicknamed "Kid" because of his youthful exuberance and ever-present smile, Gary Carter burst onto the major-league scene in 1974 as an outfielder/catcher. A two-year captain of his high school football, basketball, and baseball teams, Carter was a born leader and was named *The Sporting News*' Rookie of the Year in 1975 after belting 17 home runs and driving in 68 runs. He became the Expos' full-time catcher in 1977 and quickly established himself as one of the game's best backstops—both offensively and defensively. Carter helped lead the team to its first—and only—playoff appearance in 1981.

GARY CARTER
CATCHER

STATS

Expos seasons: 1974–84

Height: 6-2

Weight: 215

- **324 career HR**

- **3-time Gold Glove winner**

- **11-time All-Star**

- **2-time All-Star Game MVP**

ended with an impressive 95 victories.

The 1980 season promised to be a memorable one, and fans began chanting *Vive les Expos* ("Long live the Expos") at the very first game. With Dawson and Carter bashing home runs and Rogers and Scott Sanderson dominating opposing hitters, it seemed the Expos were ready to win their first division crown and reach the playoffs. On September 10, rookie pitcher Bill Gullickson helped Montreal's cause by striking out 18 Chicago Cubs en route to an Expos victory. Ultimately, the pennant race came down to a three-game series between the Expos and the Phillies. For the second time, Philadelphia was able to hold off the Expos by winning two out of three, postponing Montreal's playoff dreams for another year.

In 1981, the Expos were once again gunning for the playoffs. The already talented team added rookie sensation Tim "The Rock" Raines to the lineup, and the left fielder quickly established himself as an excellent leadoff hitter and base stealer. Because the 1981 season was shortened by a players' strike, it was divided into two halves. The Phillies won the first half of the season, while the Expos posted the division's best record in the second half. The Expos then defeated the Phillies in a special division playoff series, avenging the disappointing second-place finishes of the previous two years.

FIRST BASEMAN · ANDRES GALARRAGA

Andres Galarraga was a popular player throughout a career that took him to seven different major-league teams and saw him return to the game after a bout with cancer. Nicknamed "The Big Cat" for his extraordinary quickness despite his large frame, Galarraga was an incredible fielder and a solid hitter. While his best offensive seasons were with the Colorado Rockies, Galarraga never forgot the team that gave him his start in baseball. In 2002, he returned to the Expos as a part-time player, giving Montreal fans a second chance to see one of their all-time favorites in action.

STATS

Expos seasons: 1985–91, 2002

Height: 6-3

Weight: 235

- **1,425 career RBI**

- **399 career HR**

- **5-time All-Star**

- **2-time Gold Glove winner**

ANDRES GALARRAGA
FIRST BASEMAN

The Expos then moved on to play the Los Angeles Dodgers in the NL Championship Series (NLCS). In the hotly contested five-game series, the teams wound up tied 1–1 in the bottom of the ninth inning of the deciding Game 5. The Expos summoned Rogers from the bullpen to shut down the Dodgers and give his team a chance to win the game in extra innings. Unfortunately, Dodgers outfielder Rick Monday hit a Rogers slider out of the park to win the series. "It was a hanging slider," said Rogers sadly. "I wanted it to break down and away, but it didn't." While the Dodgers went on to win the World Series, Expos fans were left to speak dejectedly of the day they would always remember as "Blue Monday."

GOOD—BUT NOT GREAT

 s the 1982 season began, the city of Montreal was firmly behind its talented team. The overwhelmingly optimistic atmosphere led one hometown sportswriter to confidently declare, "We're the team of the '80s. With Carter, Dawson, Raines, and Rogers, what can go wrong?" Unfortunately, over the next couple of seasons, the Expos would find that plenty could—and would—go wrong, as a series of injuries and bad trades kept the team from reaching its true potential.

Not surprisingly, there were plenty of individual highlights, though. In 1982, first baseman Al Oliver, with a .331 average, became the first Expos player to win the NL batting title. Two years later, on April 13, 1984, legendary first baseman Pete Rose collected his 4,000th career hit in an Expos uniform and would go on to break Detroit Tigers outfielder Ty Cobb's record to become the all-time hits leader (with 4,256). In the early '80s, fireballing relief pitcher Jeff Reardon also began a string of impressive seasons as the Expos' closer. More often than not, when the Expos put a game into Reardon's hands, they won. However, from 1982 to 1986, the Expos were a mediocre squad. Every time they tried to move up in the standings, something would go wrong or a key player would succumb to injury.

Finally, Expos management decided to shake things up. The Expos traded Carter to the New York Mets before the 1985 season and brought in first baseman Andres "The Big Cat" Galarraga and veteran pitcher Dennis Martinez to fill the leadership void that Carter left behind. In 1987, the Expos went 91–71, but once again, they failed to make the postseason. A decade that had begun with so much promise ended in bitter disappointment, as Montreal remained frozen at 81–81 for the next two seasons.

TIM RAINES — "The Rock" combined rare speed, aggression, and batting skill to
become one of baseball's most dangerous leadoff hitters. In his 12 Expos seasons, he
perfected the art of base-stealing, setting a team record with 90 thefts in 1983.

As the team headed into the '90s, Galarraga emerged as its unquestioned leader. His lethal bat intimidated opposing pitchers, while his fielding prowess was incredible. Galarraga ripped line drives to all parts of the field, accumulating many extra-base hits. In 1990, The Big Cat won a Gold Glove anchoring the infield defense, and third baseman Tim Wallach's stellar defense earned him a Gold Glove of his own. The sure-handed Wallach stole many hits from opposing hitters while providing plenty for his team. The Expos finished 1990 in third place but slipped to last in 1991.

Before the 1992 season, two natives of the Dominican Republic arrived in Montreal: new manager Felipe Alou and talented young pitcher Pedro Martinez. Alou's patience and determination were just what the young, inexperienced Expos needed from a skipper, and Martinez's overpowering fastball gave the Expos an ace pitcher. The Dominican duo helped lead the team to 87 wins in 1992 and an impressive 94–68 record in 1993. Although the Expos narrowly missed the playoffs with back-to-back second-place finishes both years, the team finally appeared ready to again challenge the baseball elite for a World Series championship.

SECOND BASEMAN · DELINO DeSHIELDS

After his senior year in high school, Delino DeShields had a big decision to make—to either play college basketball at Villanova University or major league baseball for the Montreal Expos. Luckily for the Expos, he chose baseball. A left-handed hitter and a right-handed fielder, he used his lively legs to quickly advance through the Expos' minor-league system, making his major-league debut in 1990. DeShields finished in the league's top 10 in stolen bases 10 times, stealing a career-high 56 bags in 1991. After the 1993 season, DeShields was dealt to the Dodgers for pitcher Pedro Martinez.

STATS

Expos seasons: 1990–93

Height: 6-1

Weight: 170

• 1997 NL leader in triples (14)

• .268 career BA

• 463 career stolen bases

• 872 career runs scored

DELINO DeSHIELDS
SECOND BASEMAN

WASHINGTON NATIONALS

NATIONALS

ANDRES GALARRAGA

Andres Galarraga put together an unusual season in 1988, leading the NL in both hits (184) and strikeouts (153).

DENNIS MARTINEZ

EL PERFECTO

A perfect game is defined in major league baseball as a game in which a pitcher throws a complete-game victory that lasts a minimum of nine innings and in which no opposing player reaches first base. A perfect game is widely considered the pinnacle of pitching performance and is one of the most difficult feats to achieve in all of baseball—if not in any sport. Of course, a pitcher has to be at the top of his game, but he also has to rely on his defense to not make any errors and to occasionally make the great play. On July 28, 1991, Dennis "El Presidente"

Martinez of the Expos stepped on the mound to face the Los Angeles Dodgers in Dodger Stadium. From the start, Martinez had his best stuff. Inning after inning, he set the Dodgers down one after another. By the seventh inning, Dodgers fans began to realize that they might be witnessing history, and the stands began to buzz as Martinez set about recording the last nine outs. On his 95th pitch, he recorded the 27th and final out for a perfect game. Martinez became only the 13th pitcher in major-league history to record such a game.

MOISES ALOU

FROM CONTENDERS TO PRETENDERS

As the 1994 season unfolded, it became clear that the Expos were one of the teams to beat. In late June, the Atlanta Braves, a perennial playoff contender, came to town. Record-breaking crowds watched as the red-hot Expos swept the series, putting them in first place in the NL East. The team would not relinquish first place for the remainder of the season. Montreal's offense was led by a talented outfield—which included left fielder Moises Alou (Felipe's son) and burly right fielder Larry Walker. On the mound, Pedro Martinez dominated the opposition, and closer John Wettcland was always ready to save a Martinez gem or a game pitched by any other starter. The Expos began to look nearly unstoppable.

Then, on August 12, with the Expos holding a major-league-best 74–40 record, major-league players went on strike. After weeks of fruitless negotiations, the season was canceled. With that, the Expos' fate was sealed: the 1994 team would never have the chance to prove itself in the postseason. "A lot of things about the strike hurt," said Walker, "But having that great season wasted is

A quiet team leader, Moises Alou was named to the All-Star team for the first time in his career in 1994.

THIRD BASEMAN · LARRY PARRISH

A right-handed slugger, Parrish was a breath of fresh air for the Expos when he arrived in 1974. The third-sacker gave Expos fans a glimpse of the kind of young talent the team would rely on to mold itself into a winner. Parrish was a clutch hitter who had a way of turning pitchers' mistakes into majestic home runs. He improved his game every year, culminating in a 30-home-run and 82-RBI season in 1979. Although he was traded away to the Texas Rangers after the 1981 season, Parrish remained a feared hitter throughout the 1980s.

STATS

Expos seasons: 1974–81

Height: 6-3

Weight: 215

- **256 career HR**
- **992 career RBI**
- **1979 Expos Player of the Year**
- **2-time All-Star**

LARRY PARRISH
THIRD BASEMAN

something I don't think I'll ever get over."

By 1995, the Expos had lost many key players, including Wetteland, to free agency. But they still had Pedro Martinez. On June 3, 1995, he pitched nine innings of perfect baseball against the San Diego Padres in a scoreless game. Had the game ended there, he would have followed in the footsteps of former Expos pitcher Dennis Martinez, who pitched a perfect game in 1991. When Montreal scored a run in the top of the 10th inning, only 3 outs stood between Martinez and history. He lost his gem by allowing a leadoff double, but new closer Mel Rojas still saved the game for Montreal.

By 1996, Martinez was recognized as one of the best pitchers in the major leagues. In 1997, he won 17 games with a stunning earned run average (ERA) of 1.90 and 305 strikeouts—exploits that garnered him the NL Cy Young Award as the league's best pitcher. While the economics of the game had caused the small-market Expos to lose key players over the previous few seasons, they suffered their greatest loss at the end of the 1997 season when Martinez was traded to the Boston Red Sox.

Two new stars emerged in 1998, marking the beginning of a youth movement in Montreal: right fielder Vladimir Guerrero and relief pitcher Ugueth Urbina. The free-swinging Guerrero wowed fans with his rocket

LARRY WALKER

The 1994 strike signaled the end of
Larry Walker's Montreal career, as he
left town before the 1995 season.

SHORTSTOP · WIL CORDERO

Cordero was scouted in Puerto Rico and signed by the Expos at the age of 16. Four years later, in 1992, he was called up to the big leagues after the All-Star break. As a rookie, he overcame a variety of injuries to hit .302 in 45 games. In 1994, despite missing 52 games due to injury, the versatile shortstop had one of his best seasons as a major-leaguer, but he was then traded away after the 1995 season. When Cordero returned to play with the Expos and then the Nationals later in his career, he did so as a left fielder and a first baseman.

STATS

Expos seasons: 1992–95, 2002–03, 2005 (Washington Nationals)

Height: 6-2

Weight: 190

- **122 career HR**
- **566 career RBI**
- **.273 career BA**
- **1994 All-Star**

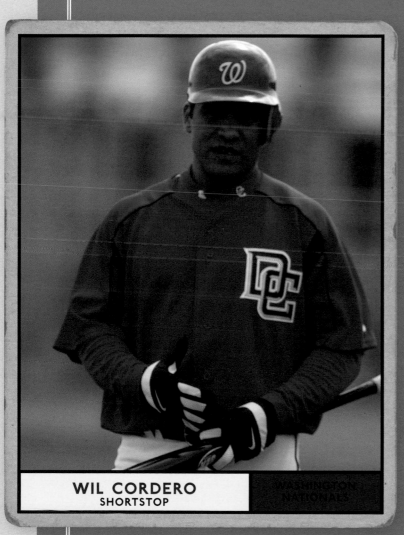

WIL CORDERO
SHORTSTOP

WASHINGTON NATIONALS

NATIONALS

[31]

LEFT FIELDER · TIM RAINES

Nicknamed "The Rock" because of his chiseled physique, Tim Raines quickly established himself as one of the game's best leadoff hitters, causing Atlanta Braves pitcher Rick Mahler to call him "the best offensive player in the league besides [Braves All-Star outfielder] Dale Murphy." In 1981, The Rock was an integral part of the only Expos team to ever make it to the postseason. In just 88 games that year, he stole an incredible 71 bases, and by 1984, he had become the first player ever to steal 70 bases in four consecutive seasons. A fan favorite, Raines was a fixture in the Expos' lineup for 12 years.

STATS

Expos seasons: 1979–90

Height: 5-8

Weight: 178

- **1987 All-Star Game MVP**

- **808 career stolen bases**

- **1,571 career runs scored**

- **7-time All-Star**

TIM RAINES
LEFT FIELDER

WASHINGTON NATIONALS

OH, CANADA!

In an attempt to increase fan interest in the game, Major League Baseball decided to add interleague games to the regular season in 1997. This meant that teams from the NL would be pitted against teams from the AL. Previously, the only times a team from the NL could meet a team from the AL were in spring training exhibition games or the World Series. When the schedule was announced, among the marquee match-ups were the New York Mets against the New York Yankees, the Chicago Cubs against the Chicago White Sox, and the Montreal Expos against the Toronto Blue Jays. For the first time ever, two big-league teams from outside the United States would be playing the game called "America's favorite pastime." For this reason, "Oh, Canada!," not the U.S. national anthem, was sung before the game. When the Blue Jays hosted the Expos on June 30, 1997, fans flooded SkyDome in Toronto to see which Canadian team was better. The Expos won the first two games by an identical 2–1 margin. The Blue Jays won the last game 7–6, but the Expos won the series, giving them bragging rights throughout Canada.

CENTER FIELDER · ANDRE DAWSON

Andre Dawson was one of the best all-around players ever to have worn a Montreal uniform. In the early 1980s, the Expos enjoyed some of their most successful seasons when "The Hawk" patrolled center field with his fast legs and sure glove. At the plate, Dawson refused to be intimidated, showing toughness by leading the league four times in being hit by pitches. When he wasn't getting plunked, he could hit home runs and steal bases with the best of them. Dawson is the only Expos player to have hit more than 200 home runs and stolen 200 bases.

STATS

Expos seasons: 1976–86

Height: 6-3

Weight: 195

- **1977 NL Rookie of the Year**
- **1987 NL MVP**
- **438 career HR**
- **8-time All-Star**

ANDRE DAWSON
CENTER FIELDER

WASHINGTON NATIONALS

throwing arm and explosive bat. "He has all the tools to be outstanding, especially that arm," said Expos general manager Jim Beattie. "That's what people 'ooh' and 'ahh' about." Meanwhile, Urbina was a dominant pitcher who seemed to enjoy the high-pressure situations often presented in the ninth inning. His 100-mile-per-hour fastball enabled him to save more than 100 games in his first 3 seasons. Unfortunately, the rest of the team's young players struggled, and the Expos finished fourth in the NL East in 1998 and 1999.

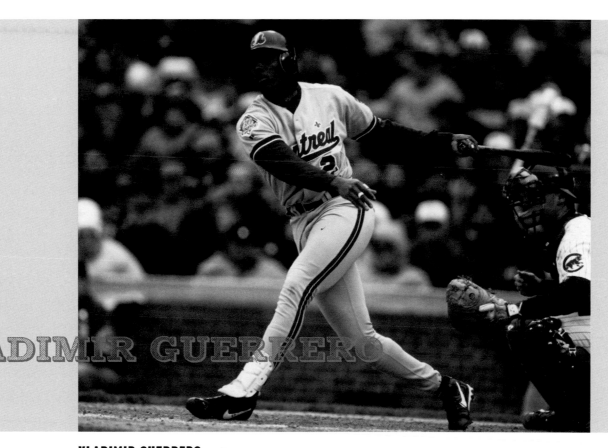

VLADIMIR GUERRERO – Guerrero was known as baseball's best "bad ball" hitter, able to make solid contact with pitches thrown well outside the strike zone. The slugger was also unique among major-leaguers in that he hit barehanded, without batting gloves.

THE END OF AN ERA

The Expos' youthful club continued to stumble in the new century, despite boasting such players as slick-fielding shortstop Orlando Cabrera, second baseman Jose Vidro, and hard-throwing pitcher Javier Vazquez—who quickly became the anchor of the club's pitching staff. The team's youth and inconsistency led to an abundance of losses, which cost Alou his job as manager. When Jeff Torborg took over as skipper, his mission was to return the Expos to respectability, but it was to be a long, winding road back.

Five consecutive losing seasons had hurt the team's ability to draw fans, which was causing the franchise to lose money. After the 2001 season, rumors began to spread that Major League Baseball might contract, or eliminate, two teams. The Expos and the Minnesota Twins, two of the least profitable clubs, seemed likely candidates. Even though the threats of contraction never materialized, Major League Baseball officials took over ownership of the Expos and soon hired Omar Minaya as baseball's first-ever Latino general manager and Frank Robinson as the club's manager. While many wondered whether the Expos would stay in Montreal, Minaya and Robinson never doubted they could improve the team.

Orlando Cabrera was most valued for his fielding but was also a key run producer, posting 96 RBI in 2001.

Guererro and Vidro helped the Expos get off to a hot start in 2002. With a division title within reach, Minaya pulled off a tremendous trade, bringing in standout pitcher Bartolo Colón, who went 10–4 with a 3.31 ERA for the Expos. A month later, Minaya pulled off another deal, bringing veteran outfielder Cliff Floyd back to the team. The renewed Expos battled the Atlanta Braves for the NL East title deep into the season before fading to an 83–79 finish— their first winning season in five years.

In 2003, the Expos were once again a formidable opponent. Robinson's no-nonsense approach to the game established a winning attitude for both rookies and veterans, and a trade for pitcher Livan Hernandez gave Montreal an extra boost. The Expos' modest success on the field (83–79) did not translate into fan interest, though, and when they lost Guerrero to free agency after the season, they were destined to take a tumble in the standings. As a result, baseball officials announced that the Expos would move after the 2004 season. On October 3, 2004, Montreal lost to the New York Mets, 8–1, in the last game of the season. It was the last game the team known as the Expos would ever play. "I know it's the last ballgame as the Montreal Expos, but I know it's not the last ballgame," said Robinson. "I'll be managing with most of these ballplayers [next year]."

SAN JUAN EXPOS

In 2001, the small-market Expos found themselves unable to compete financially with teams in bigger metropolitan areas such as New York, Chicago, and Los Angeles. As a result, Montreal fans found it difficult to support their losing team. In 2001, the Expos routinely drew fewer than 10,000 fans per game, averaging a woeful 7,935 fans for home games. Whispers that two teams would be contracted (or eliminated), swirled throughout the majors. The Montreal Expos and the Minnesota Twins (another small-market team) appeared to be the leading candidates for contraction. On February 14, 2002, the league agreed not to contract any teams. Still, Major League Baseball looked into alternative ways to improve the Expos' attendance and revenue. In 2003, the team announced it would play 22 of its "home games" at Hiram Bithorn Stadium in San Juan, Puerto Rico. Fans in Puerto Rico flocked to the small stadium, largely to see the team's Latino stars, such as Vladimir Guerrero and Jose Vidro. The games played in San Juan regularly outdrew the games played in Montreal. Thanks in large part to the games played in San Juan, the Expos were able to draw more than a million fans at "home" for the first time since 1998.

NATIONALS

[39]

RIGHT FIELDER · VLADIMIR GUERRERO

When Guerrero made his major-league debut in 1996, his raw skills included a superb throwing arm, speed, and rare slugging power. Still, many doubted that he would become a star because of his free-swinging approach at the plate. But Guerrero proved to his doubters that he could get hold of almost any pitch thrown to him. By 1998, he had established himself as one of the game's rising stars, and from then through 2003, he led the Expos in most offensive categories. After an injury-shortened 2003 season, Guerrero signed a free agent contract with the Los Angeles Angels of Anaheim.

STATS

Expos seasons: 1996–2003

Height: 6-2

Weight: 218

- 338 career HR

- .325 career BA

- 2004 AL MVP

- 7-time All-Star

VLADIMIR GUERRERO
RIGHT FIELDER

A NEW BEGINNING

By the time the 2005 season began, the Montreal Expos had been transformed into the Washington Nationals. The return of baseball to the capital of the United States was a resounding success. Washington, D.C., had been home to a major-league franchise called the Washington Senators from 1901 until 1971, and after a nearly 40-year drought, its baseball-starved citizens were ready to root for a new team. Still, not much was expected of Robinson's squad, especially after the Nationals lost the season opener, 8–4, to the Philadelphia Phillies. "There wasn't no pageantry today for the D.C. Nationals," said reliever Joey Eischen. "We came here to kick some butt—and we didn't. But we'll be out there again on Wednesday, and we're going to bring it."

After losing that first game, the team "brought it" to the rest of the NL, soon sprinting to first place in the NL East. The off-season acquisition of right fielder Jose Guillen, who finished the year with 24 home runs, provided a middle-of-the-lineup threat to opposing pitchers. While promising rookie outfielder Ryan Church helped carry the offensive load, workhorse Livan Hernandez won 15 games and led the major leagues in innings pitched. Perhaps the biggest surprise was closer Chad Cordero. As a second-year player,

Livan Hernandez gave Washington championship experience, having won a World Series
with the Florida Marlins in 1997.

CHAD CORDERO

Chad Cordero used pinpoint accuracy rather than great throwing speed to become one of baseball's top closers.

expectations for Cordero were modest, but he blazed his way to a league-leading 47 saves.

As the season unfolded, the Nationals remained in the playoff hunt. Robinson continually got the most out of and expected the best from his team, preaching good fundamental play. For most of the 2005 season, the Expos struggled to score runs, but a mixture of good defense, pitching, and timely hitting enabled them to win many close games. With only two weeks left, the Nationals remained within striking distance of the NL Wild

MANAGER · FELIPE ALOU

The Alou family was a baseball family. Felipe, along with younger brothers Jesús and Matty, began his major-league career with the San Francisco Giants, where the Alous made up the first all-brother outfield in 1959. After his playing days ended, Alou worked his way up the coaching ranks until 1992, when he was hired as the Expos' manager. Under Alou's guidance, the Expos became World Series contenders during the early 1990s, and Alou became the winningest manager in club history. After leaving Montreal in 2001, he went on to manage the Giants.

STATS

Expos seasons as manager: 1992–2001

Height: 6-0

Weight: 195

Managerial Record: 1,033–1,021

FELIPE ALOU
MANAGER

WASHINGTON NATIONALS

YOUNG GUNS

Most fans come to the ballpark hoping to see base hits, runs, and, if they're lucky, maybe a home run or two. Other fans, often baseball purists, appreciate an old-fashioned pitchers' duel. When two pitchers at the top of their game face off, runs are hard to come by. On April 9, 2003, two of the game's up-and-coming starting pitchers squared off at Wrigley Field in Chicago. The Expos' Javier Vazquez and the Cubs' Mark Prior were each looking to make their mark on the game. In the second inning, Vazquez gave up a two-out, two-run home run to Cubs catcher Damian Miller. Then,

Vazquez settled down and began to notch strikeout after strikeout. Meanwhile, Prior was sending the Expos back to the dugout with relative ease as well. The afternoon would belong to the two pitchers. Before leaving after the seventh inning, Vazquez struck out an incredible 14 batters—an average of two batters per inning! Unfortunately for Vazquez, Prior pitched a complete-game, four-hit shutout—striking out 12 Expos. For the record, Vazquez lost the game 3–0, and Prior won it. But the real winners were the nearly 30,000 fans who witnessed the exciting duel.

Card playoff spot. Even after the Houston Astros ran away with the Wild Card berth, the Nationals remained one of the game's best success stories of 2005. "I think we did what we had to do to capture the imagination of the D.C. fans," Robinson said.

Unfortunately, 2006 was a less-inspiring season. Slugging outfielder Alfonso Soriano wowed the hometown fans by slugging 46 home runs, but the club ended with a 71–91 record, then said goodbye to both Soriano and Vidro. Without these veterans, most experts predicted an even worse 2007 season in Washington. Fans hoped that a new generation of young players—including Cordero, third baseman Ryan Zimmerman, first baseman Nick Johnson, and outfielder Austin Kearns—would prove the experts wrong as the team prepared to move into the new Nationals Ballpark in 2008. Zimmerman showed the most potential of the bunch in 2006, slugging 20 homers with 110 runs batted in (RBI).

The Montreal Expos had their share of ups and downs but still provided their fans with heroes, from dominant pitchers such as Steve Rogers to power hitters such as Vladimir Guerrero. Now known as the Washington Nationals and led by players such as Ryan Zimmerman and Chad Cordero, the franchise is aiming to bring its first World Series title to its new home in the nation's capital.

NATIONALS